Ad...
Hidden Haven Ranch

LEARNING ABOUT PRAYER AS A FAMILY

By
Mary E. Erickson

Writing For Children
Mary E. Erickson
761 Grey Eagle Circle South
Colorado Springs, CO 80919

Cover art and other illustrations:
  Richard Jesse Watson

Scripture quotations in this publication
are from the *Holy Bible: New International
Version* (NIV). Copyright 1973, 1978, 1984,
International Bible Society. Used by per-
mission of Zondervan Bible publishers.
Other versions used are *The Living Bible* (TLB),
copyright 1971 by Tyndale House Publishers,
Wheaton, IL, used by permission; and
The King James Version (KJV).

The Lord's Prayer on pages 140-142 is
taken from Matthew 6:9-13 (KJV).

Printed in the United States of America

First Printing 1989, by NavPress
Second Printing 1993, by Banta Company
Third Printing 1993, by Banta Company

CONTENTS

Note to Parents 7
WHAT IS PRAYER?
    1. Welcome to Hidden Haven Ranch 11
    2. Prayer Is More Than Asking 19
PRAISING
    3. Complimenting God 27
    4. Aunt Marta's Method 31
    5. Log Church in the Rockies 39
THANKING
    6. Thanks for Fish and Fun and Feelings 47
    7. Thanks for Rainy Days Too 55
    8. Cockleburs and Currycombs 61
CONFESSING
    9. Breaking Ranch Rules 69
    10. Lost in the Mountains 75
    11. A Cow, a Calf, and a Nagging Conscience 79
ASKING FOR OTHERS
    12. Rodeo Riders 89
    13. Becoming a Go-Between 95
    14. Secrets Around a Campfire 101
ASKING FOR SELF
    15. Green Eyes in the Barn 111
    16. Short Prayers Count Too 117
    17. A Challenge at the County Fair 123
PUTTING IT ALL TOGETHER
    18. Crutches Aren't Forever 133
    19. The Perfect Example 139
    20. Goodbye, Summer 145

> And this I pray, that your love may abound still more and more in real knowledge and all discernment, so that you may approve the things that are excellent, in order to be sincere and blameless until the day of Christ.
> I Philippians 1:9,10

Dear Friends,

Does your child know how to pray? Can there be any more important skill than knowing how to communicate with our Creator and Savior? For many families, and children in particular, prayer has become a dry "wish-list" with inconsistent "results."

In *Adventure at Hidden Haven Ranch* your family will learn about prayer as you follow Ryan's adventures at his uncle's ranch in Colorado.

We hope your family will find this book exciting to read. More than that, we hope it inspires each member to learn how to talk to God, personally!

With our compliments,
THE TIMBERDOODLE

AUTHOR

Mary Erickson has been enthusiastically involved with children and teenagers all her adult life. As a pastor's wife for fifteen years, she invested her time in youth, teaching Sunday school classes and directing children's churches and choirs, daily vacation Bible schools, and summer camps. She also spent four years teaching in Seoul, South Korea. She occasionally travels with her husband, the President of Compassion International, to other countries where over 100,000 children are learning about Jesus while they study reading, writing, and arithmetic.

As a parent, Mary is the mother of three and grandmother of four. As a teacher for eleven years, she taught in elementary school, junior high, and high school. As an author, she specializes in writing for children. She has written *Jesus the Wonder-Worker* series for eight- to ten-year-olds and *Six Busy Days* for four- to seven-year olds.

NOTE TO PARENTS

Sometimes the task and responsibility of molding and training children entrusted to our care is overwhelming. We wonder how we can influence them for good and for God in this environment. I've felt that way. That's one reason why I wrote this book, which helps Christian parents teach their children how to pray.

Adventure at Hidden Haven Ranch is meant to be an entertaining and instructional book for family devotions. The book, along with a few additional items listed at the end of each chapter, teaches children, ages seven to twelve, how to talk to God.

This family devotional project can be completed in two months, if you meet about three times a week. Each chapter is an exciting adventure with Ryan at his uncle's ranch in Colorado.

At the close of each chapter, you'll find an activity page divided into three parts: (1) a Bible verse "To

Think About"; (2) questions and ideas "To Talk About"; (3) activities "To Do." The main activity is making prayer cards based on the five elements of prayer (praising, thanking, confessing, asking for others, and asking for self).

While the paramount purpose of the book is to help children learn how to compose their own prayers, I believe you'll find that the book generates and encourages deep discussions. It also contributes to the character building and spiritual growth of family members.

May you find help and hope as Christian parents in the weeks ahead, and may you and your children more deeply experience the exciting privilege of talking to God.

WHAT IS PRAYER?

Chapter 1

WELCOME TO HIDDEN HAVEN RANCH

The Jeep rounded the last horseshoe loop and headed for the ranch.

Ryan Simpson was speechless. Taking hold of the frame of the open Jeep, he pulled himself up. The wind blew his stubborn, straw-colored hair up and away from his face.

Before him lay Hidden Haven Ranch. The rolling green valley stretched out for miles. Down the middle meandered the Weminuche Creek, fed by melting snow from the Colorado Rocky Mountains.

Ryan whistled in wonderment. The houses and barns looked like toys. So did the horses and cows grazing in the pastures. Beyond the valley he saw tall ponderosa pines and the snow-covered peaks of the mountains in the San Juan National Forest.

Sitting back down, Ryan said, "You picked a perfect name for your ranch, Uncle Grady. I'm lucky, getting to spend my summer here."

Uncle Grady steered around a fallen rock in the road. He was a husky man with broad shoulders. His ruddy face always wore a wide smile.

"It'll be different than coming for two weeks with your family. But I don't think you'll get bored. There's plenty to do."

"Like horseback riding, hiking and exploring, fishing, watching a rodeo." Ryan sighed with delight.

"All that and more." Uncle Grady stopped the Jeep at the ranch gate. "I intend to put you to work." He slapped Ryan on the knee. "But working on a ranch in Colorado will be fun. Not like taking trash out in a suburb of Chicago."

Ryan ran to the gate and held it open until Uncle Grady drove through. Settling back in the Jeep, Ryan said, "I can hardly wait to ride Rustler."

"You won't have to wait long."

Riding across the meadow came Pete O'Neill, Uncle Grady's ranching partner. He rode the sorrel quarter horse to Ryan's side of the Jeep.

Pete's dark eyes were friendly. His short reddish-brown beard covered his jaws clear to his sideburns. His shaggy hair barely touched his collar. Ryan admired him because he was six feet tall and all muscle.

Tipping his battered straw hat, Pete said, "Welcome to Hidden Haven Ranch."

"Hi, Pete."

Reaching out, Ryan scratched the blaze on Rustler's face. "Hi, old boy. Did you miss me?"

Rustler neighed noisily.

"Grady tells me you're going to be in charge of Rustler this summer," Pete said.

"Really?" Ryan's blue eyes opened wide.

Uncle Grady winked. Ryan noticed that he still scrunched up his nose, wrinkled his cheek, and

13

wiggled his dark moustache whenever he winked.

Ryan winked back.

"Would you like to take charge now?" asked Pete.

"You bet!" Ryan tripped over his own feet getting out of the Jeep. "I hope I didn't forget how to ride."

"It'll all come back to you when you hit the saddle." Pete shortened the stirrups to fit Ryan's legs. "Hey! You've grown quite a bit since last year. That's great, 'cause cowboys need long legs."

Holding the reins securely, Ryan shoved his toes into the stirrups. With his tongue pressed against the roof of his mouth, he made a clicking sound. Rustler obeyed, trotting toward the barn.

At the corral, Ryan dismounted. He looped the reins over the fence rail. "This is going to be my best summer ever," he said, patting Rustler on the neck.

On the back porch Aunt Marta waited, neat and trim in her blue jeans. Her short brown hair covered her ears and curved gently under, hugging her neck. Her warm smile matched Uncle Grady's.

"Oh, Ryan, I'm glad you could come," she said, squeezing him so tightly he lost his breath.

The country kitchen was just as Ryan remembered—filled with cheerfulness and the aroma of freshly baked bread. The table was set, and dinner was waiting.

Long after the apple pie was gone and the moon was high in the sky, Ryan sat on the creaky porch

14

swing with his aunt and uncle. They took turns talking and listening until all three began yawning.

"It's time to say good night," announced Uncle Grady. "Working cowboys can't sleep till noon."

Aunt Marta showed Ryan his room. She folded the blanket back and fluffed the pillows. "Good night," she said, patting his cheek. "Sweet dreams."

Ryan watched her leave the room. She was a nice aunt, but he wished she'd stop patting him on the cheek. After all, he wasn't a kid anymore.

Ryan emptied his blue backpack and luggage. He hung his new plaid shirt in the closet. He liked the Western style with snaps instead of buttons. Mom had given it to him as an early birthday present. He'd be eleven next week.

Among his T-shirts he found a pink envelope. Opening the note, he read: "Son, I love you and will miss you. Have fun, but remember to do your share of the work. And don't forget to say your prayers. Love, Mom."

"Say your prayers!" Mom always says that, thought Ryan. *Why should I? I never get what I ask for.* But he obediently knelt beside his bed, clasped his hands under his chin, and closed his eyes.

"Dear God," he began. "Remember me? You still haven't given me the bicycle I asked for. I need it before school starts. All my friends have bicycles. Amen." He finished in one breath.

With nothing to do but fall asleep, Ryan had some time to think.

Mom always says that prayer changes things. And Dad said he prayed when he needed a new job, and he found one. Prayer seems to work for other people, but it doesn't work for me. Is there something wrong with the way I'm praying?

Ryan lay awake a long time before he finally drifted off to sleep.

TO THINK ABOUT

Do not be anxious about anything, but in everything, by prayer and petition, with thanksgiving, present your requests to God. (Philippians 4:6)

TO TALK ABOUT

1. In the Bible verse above, the Apostle Paul tells us how to pray.
   a. In what way did Ryan follow Paul's advice?
   b. How did Ryan fail to obey the Scripture?
2. What do you think Ryan meant by "prayer"?
3. How did Ryan act when he was in God's presence (when he prayed)?

TO DO

Ryan is going to work on a special project during his vacation. If you want to do it too, you'll need some supplies. Perhaps you can find them around the house. You may need to buy a few items. Each family member will need the following:

- a Bible (two people can share one)
- pen or pencil
- five rubber bands or large paper clips
- 3" x 5" lined index cards (at least thirty-five per person)
- small box (stationery, greeting card, or shoe box)
- paper to decorate your box (gift-wrapping paper and glue, or contact paper)

The family may share the following items:

- crayons or felt markers with wide tips
- a dictionary
- a notebook to write down definitions or comments

Chapter 2

PRAYER IS MORE THAN ASKING

Ryan awakened the next morning to the smell of bacon frying and biscuits baking.

He stuck his long legs into his faded blue jeans. He smiled as he noticed how much sock showed between his jeans and his sneakers. *I'm getting taller*, he thought.

Wetting his stubborn hair, he combed it back off his forehead. In the mirror he saw his pale skin and freckles. Spending this summer in the sun would change that. He'd like the tan, but he groaned when he thought of bigger, browner freckles.

As Ryan came to the breakfast table, Aunt Marta was just taking the bacon out of the frying pan. "Good morning," she said. "Did you have a good sleep?"

"Oh, sort of, I guess," Ryan said. He thought back

to his question about prayer.

When Ryan, Aunt Marta, and Uncle Grady were all seated around the table, Uncle Grady turned to Ryan. "Would you say grace for us?"

Ryan bowed his head and closed his eyes. "God is great. God is good. And we thank Him for this food. Amen," Ryan recited. *That sounds dumb*, he thought, *like a two-year-old. I'm going to be learning a lot of things here this summer. I wonder if I could learn how to pray too.*

Ryan took a deep breath. "Aunt Marta, Uncle Grady, I know this sounds kind of dumb, but could you teach me how to pray?"

"I don't think that sounds dumb at all," said Uncle Grady. "It took me a long time to learn about prayer." He reached for the Bible that was always close at hand on a shelf in the kitchen. Opening the Bible, he handed it to Ryan. "Read Luke 11:1."

Ryan read: "One day Jesus was praying in a certain place. When he finished, one of his disciples said to him, 'Lord teach us to pray, just as John taught his disciples.'"

"Grown-ups asked for help," said Uncle Grady, "and Jesus taught them how to pray. Your aunt and I will be happy to teach you this summer."

Aunt Marta carried the dishes to the kitchen sink. "What do you think prayer is, Ryan?"

"Asking God for things."

"That's what many people believe," Aunt Marta said. "But it's more than that. Asking for something is only one part of prayer."

Uncle Grady added, "I think of prayer as simply talking to God—about anything, anytime, anywhere."

"Through prayer we worship God," said Aunt Marta. "So prayer is more than words. It's the way we feel toward God. Our attitude is important when we talk to Him."

Aunt Marta brought to the table a woodcarving of praying hands. Placing the woodcarving in front of Ryan, she said, "Just as the hand has five fingers, prayer has five parts. Before the summer is over, we'll discuss these five ingredients, and as we talk about them you'll learn how to put them together to make a prayer that pleases God."

"Okay," Ryan said.

"Let's start with the thumb," continued Aunt Marta. "It's the most important part of your hand. Without your thumb, your other fingers wouldn't be able to do much. In prayer, the thumb stands for . . ."

"Help! Grady, I need help!" yelled Pete, banging on the screen door. "It's the brown mare. She's thrashing about in the barn."

Grabbing his straw hat from the rack by the door, Grady called over his shoulder. "Come along, Ryan. Ginger will need lots of help. She's having trouble giving birth to her first foal."

TO THINK ABOUT

I will meditate on all your works
and consider all your mighty deeds.
Your ways, O God, are holy.
What god is so great as our God?
You are the God who performs miracles;
you display your power among the peoples.
(Psalm 77:12-14)

TO TALK ABOUT

1. *Meditate* means to think carefully and seriously about something. To meditate you must put everything else out of your mind and concentrate on one idea.

   Pretend your family went hiking in the mountains and decided to take a picture. Through the camera lens, you saw a stream, trees, and mountains. But you narrowed the focus and took a picture of one yellow daisy. How is meditating like that?
2. Aunt Marta said our attitude is important when we talk to God. How will knowing what Psalm 77:12-14 says help our attitude?
3. Ryan assumed praying was easy, so he was ashamed to ask someone to teach him to pray. Why should he *not* be ashamed?
4. How do you think Ryan will define prayer now that he's learned more about it?

TO DO

Prepare your "Prayer Project" box to hold the cards you'll be making. You may cover your box with the contact or wrapping paper, put your name on it, and decorate it.

PRAISING

Chapter 3

COMPLIMENTING GOD

Three hours after Ryan, Uncle Grady, and Pete reached the barn, they watched Ginger, the brown mare, bathe her newborn foal. With her tongue, Ginger washed the foal's face and licked his wet hair until it lay smooth and shiny.

When the bath was finished, Ginger gently nudged the foal. Finally he stood and wobbled around the stall.

"I can't believe it!" said Ryan. "He's only a few hours old and he can walk already."

"God planned it that way," explained Uncle Grady. "If baby animals are going to survive in this world, they have to be able to stand up and move about as soon as they're born."

When Ginger stood up, the foal quickly found his mother's milk and began sucking rhythmically.

Ryan wrinkled his forehead. "How does he know where to find food?"

"That's another of God's ideas," answered Uncle Grady. "God created all babies—both human and animal—with the instinct to suck. They need nourishment instantly. There's no time to take lessons."

"Talking about food, I think I need some," Ryan said. "My stomach's sending out an S.O.S."

Looking at his watch, Uncle Grady said, "It's past noon. I bet Marta has lunch ready."

At the kitchen table, Ryan talked while he shoveled food into his mouth. "The kids back home will never believe me when I tell them I actually saw a baby horse being born. God must like animals a lot. He sure planned things just perfect for them."

"You've already learned the first ingredient of prayer, Ryan." Aunt Marta held up her thumb. "Remember what I was telling you at breakfast? This stands for praise. You're offering God praise when you tell how good God is."

"You mean when I begin a prayer, I should give God a compliment?" Ryan asked.

Uncle Grady chuckled and nodded. "Well, that's one way to think about praise. We often compliment people we care about. I tell Marta what a wonderful wife she is."

Reaching for another crispy-fried drumstick, Ryan said, "And I tell her she's a terrific cook."

Aunt Marta beamed. "I must admit I love compliments. In fact, I need them like the wheat needs the rain." She pushed her dark hair behind her ears. "Praise makes people happy."

"Praise pleases God, too, and it brings honor to His name," Uncle Grady added. "Psalm 135:3 says, 'Praise the LORD, for the LORD is good; sing praise to his name, for that is pleasant.'"

"I don't think I've ever told God anything like that when I prayed," Ryan said honestly. "I didn't know it was important."

"Neither did I," said Aunt Marta, "until I started studying about prayer. Now I like to think of praise as the key that opens the door to God's presence."

Uncle Grady pushed back his chair and picked up his hat. "I've got to get back to the barn and see how the spotted colt is doing. Anyone want to come along?"

"Sure do," said Ryan. Passing the coat rack, he grabbed the shabby cowboy hat Uncle Grady had loaned him. If it hadn't been for Ryan's large ears, the hat would have fallen over his eyes. But Ryan didn't care. It made him feel like a real cowboy.

TO THINK ABOUT

Through Jesus, therefore, let us continually offer to God a sacrifice of praise—the fruit of lips that confess his name. . . . For with such sacrifices God is pleased. (Hebrews 13:15-16)

TO TALK ABOUT

1. a. What is the first ingredient of prayer, pictured by the thumb?
   b. How did Aunt Marta define it?
   c. How did Ryan define it?
2. *Sacrifice* is an act of offering something precious to God. In Old Testament times, priests offered animals as a sacrifice to God. Read Psalm 69:30-31. What pleases God more than offering a bull or an ox?
3. *Fruits*, like apples and strawberries, are the product of a tree or plant.
   a. What is the fruit of your lips?
   b. What kind of fruit pleases God?
4. Read Psalm 36:6-7. Name some animals and tell how God planned for their survival.

TO DO

In the next get-together, you will begin making prayer cards with Ryan. Do you have your box and all your supplies ready?

Chapter 4
AUNT MARTA'S METHOD

"Ginger and her colt are sleeping," said Ryan, looking into the barn stall.

"Both worked hard this morning," Uncle Grady said. "They need to rest."

Ryan sighed in disappointment. "So, what're we going to do?"

"I've got a good job for you. Colorado's bright sun sucks the moisture out of leather. Makes it brittle. Come to the tack room, and I'll teach you how to protect saddles."

With water and saddle soap, Ryan and his uncle cleaned the saddles and reins.

"What's next?" Ryan asked.

Uncle Grady handed Ryan a clean cloth and a small can of oil. "Now we rub neat's-foot oil into the leather to soften and preserve it."

Pouring oil onto the cloth, Ryan rubbed it into the leather. When the job became routine, his mind started to wander. His thoughts roamed from cowboy chores to summer sports back home.

"Would this oil be good for my baseball mitt?" asked Ryan, disturbing the long silence.

"You bet it will." Grady grinned. "The oil will keep your glove soft and molded to your hand, helping you scoop up grounders and wrap around high flies."

"I'll miss summer baseball," Ryan said gloomily.

Uncle Grady plunked down another saddle between them. "Tell me about your team."

Ryan told about the games his team had won last year, before a clanging cowbell interrupted them.

"What's that?" asked Ryan.

"It's quitting time. We have thirty minutes to finish our job and wash up for dinner."

That night Ryan ate two servings of everything, even the cauliflower. As he was pressing his fork into the last chocolate cake crumb, Uncle Grady reached for the Bible he kept on a shelf in the kitchen.

Turning to Psalm 100:4, Uncle Grady said, "Here's a verse that tells us how to approach God when we pray."

Ryan read the verse out loud: "Enter his gates with thanksgiving and his courts with praise; give thanks to him and praise his name."

"Praise is telling about the worth or value of someone," Aunt Marta said. "Remember the prayer you say at mealtime: 'God is great. God is good . . .'?"

Ryan nodded.

"You were praising God; you just didn't realize it."

Uncle Grady added, "In *The Living Bible*, Psalm 107:31 tells us to praise the Lord for His goodness and His wonderful works, so Marta and I praise God for who God is and what He has made and done."

"Start with what you know," suggested Aunt Marta.

Ryan thought for a minute. "I remember the first verse I memorized in vacation Bible school: 'God loved us and sent His Son.'"

"That's good. Praise God for His love and for sending Jesus to save us. How about another?"

"In the beginning God created the heavens and the earth," Ryan recited.

"That tells us God is the great Creator," said Uncle Grady. "What else did He make?"

"Day and night, sun and stars, birds and . . . Wow!" Ryan exclaimed.

In her desk Aunt Marta found three pencils and some white 3″ x 5″ index cards. "Here's a project we can work on this summer. Whenever we find something to praise God for, we'll write it on a card."

"You be first," Ryan said to his uncle. "I'll watch."

"My favorite praise verse is Revelation 4:8. I'll

rewrite that in my own words."

> PRAISING
>
> Lord God Almighty, You are holy, pure and perfect in every way. Everything You do is right and good.
>
> Revelation 4:8

"The Psalms are full of praise," said Aunt Marta. "I'm going to rewrite Psalm 95:3-5." She wrote:

> PRAISING
>
> The Lord is a great God.
> He is the King above all gods.
> The mountain peaks belong to God.
> The sea is His, for He made it.
>
> Psalm 95:3-5

"I want to make a card about John 3:16," Ryan said. He wrote:

PRAISING
Dear God, You loved the world
so much You sent Your only Son
to take away our sins so we
can live with You forever.
John 3:16

"Now I'm going to write about the new colt," Ryan said.

PRAISING
Dear God, You're a terrific
Creator. You made newborn
animals know how to walk
and find milk.

"Does that sound right?" Ryan asked.

"God doesn't care if we use important-sounding words," Uncle Grady replied. "But He does care if we use sincere words. I think you're a fast learner!"

"Thanks." Ryan's broad grin stretched his freckles. "Aunt Marta was right. Praise makes a person feel good."

TO THINK ABOUT

Great and marvelous are your deeds,
Lord God Almighty.
Just and true are your ways,
King of the ages. (Revelation 15:3)

TO TALK ABOUT
1. What did Uncle Grady say he praises God for?
2. In Revelation 15:3, find two phrases that tell who God is. What does *almighty* mean? (A dictionary might help.)
3. Find one line in the verse that praises God for what He has done. What are some of God's "deeds" you have read or heard about?
4. What does *just and true are your ways* mean?

TO DO
Make prayer cards, as Ryan did.
1. On the top line of a 3″ x 5″ card, print in capital letters PRAISING.

2. Tell who God is, or what God has done, or what God has made. You may want to do one of the following:

   a. Copy a card made by Ryan, his aunt or uncle.

   b. Copy one of these Bible verses, or write it in your own words.

      • Genesis 1:21,25

      • Psalm 77:13-14

      • Psalm 86:5,8,10,15

      • Isaiah 40:28-29

3. Use your prayer box to store your cards and supplies.

Chapter 5

LOG CHURCH IN THE ROCKIES

Ryan liked Sundays in the mountains. Worshiping in the old log church made him feel like a pioneer. He wished he could have helped cut down the lodgepole pines, split and notch them, and build this church— or the pulpit. It also was made of rough-hewn pine. So was the cross behind it.

Gazing out the window, Ryan saw lavender columbines, white bark of aspens, tall pine trees, rugged mountains, and blue sky. He couldn't help but think about God.

Ryan was sitting on the third pew beside Kevin Bennett, his best Colorado friend.

Kevin's wavy brown hair flopped on his forehead, giving him a casual look. Everything about Kevin was casual. He was a fun-loving fifth-grader who wore a

39

mischievous expression most of the time.

Kevin opened the hymnal to page 40, and the boys sang along with the congregation.

To God be the glory—great things He hath done!
So loved He the world that He gave us His Son,
Who yielded His life an atonement for sin,
And opened the lifegate that all may go in.

That sounds like the Praising Card I made, thought Ryan. *I've sung this song before. But I never thought much about the words.*

Ryan joined in on the chorus.

Praise the Lord, praise the Lord,
Let the earth hear His voice!
Praise the Lord, praise the Lord,
Let the people rejoice!
O come to the Father thru Jesus the Son,
And give Him the glory—great things He hath
    done!

The words had new meaning for Ryan this time. He was praising God, and the praise was bubbling up from deep inside him.

Pastor Olson stood up behind the pulpit. Ryan wondered if he could possibly be as old as the church building. The top of his head was bald and shiny, but just above his ears there was a wide band of snowy white hair. He was short and stout, and his face was round and kind.

He announced, "The theme of our worship service today is praising God."

Ryan glanced at his uncle in the choir. Uncle Grady winked in his usual way. *I'll have to teach Uncle Grady how to wink without wrecking his face*, thought Ryan.

"Open your Bibles to Psalm 103," said the pastor.

Kevin found Psalms in the pew Bible, and let Ryan look at it with him.

The pastor read from the *King James Version.* "Bless the LORD, O my soul: and all that is within me, bless his holy name. Bless the LORD, O my soul, and forget not all his benefits."

Looking over the top of his wire-rimmed glasses, the pastor said, "You may ask, 'What does it mean to bless the Lord? I thought it was the Lord who blesses us.' That's true! But the word *bless* has several meanings."

Pastor Olson walked to the side of the pulpit. "When God blesses us, it means that He gives us happiness or success."

Pastor Olson paced to the other side of the pulpit and seemed to look directly at the boys in the third pew. "But in these verses, it says *we* are to bless God. That means *we* are to worship, adore, and glorify Him. In

41

other words, praise Him."

I know what praise is, Ryan thought. *It's telling how good God is.*

The pastor continued. "Next, the verse tells us how to praise God: 'And all that is within me, bless his holy name.' That means with all your soul, with all your heart, with all your mind, and with all your strength."

Someone behind Ryan said emphatically, "A-men!"

"Now, let's move on to verse 2. It tells us what to praise God for."

Ryan followed in the Bible.

"'Forget not all his benefits.' Do you know what a benefit is? It's something that's for your good. It's something that improves your situation. Let's see what these benefits are."

Ryan read several verses to himself. *Here's an idea for making Praising Cards*, he thought.

Soon he grew tired of reading, so he looked at the maps in the back of the Bible. He loved maps. The one of Paul's missionary journeys fascinated him. He didn't hear another word the pastor said until Kevin poked him in the ribs.

"Hey, Ryan," whispered Kevin. "Church is over."

After dinner Ryan said, "That was a good sermon. I got some ideas for making Praising Cards. The verse I like said God is patient and doesn't get mad very easy. I'd like to put that on a card." Ryan printed:

PRAISING
I praise You, Lord, because You
are so good and kind. You are
very patient, slow to get
angry, and full of love.
                    Psalm 103:8

"Verses 3 and 4 tell what God has done," said
Aunt Marta. "I'll make a card from them."

PRAISING
O God, You are the Great Physician.
You heal my body. Your love and
tender mercies surround me.
                    Psalm 103:3-4

Uncle Grady made a Praising Card from verse 5

about God as the Great Provider. When he finished, he gave it to Ryan. "Add this to your stack. It'll help you remember about blessings and benefits."

"I know," said Ryan with a smile. "When God gives the benefits, I should give the blessings."

TO THINK ABOUT

How good it is to sing praises to our God, how pleasant and fitting to praise him! (Psalm 147:1)

TO TALK ABOUT

1. Psalm 147:1 says that praising God is good for two reasons. What are they?
2. What did Pastor Olson say a benefit is?
3. How can you "bless the Lord"?
4. What are some benefits from God that you could praise Him for?

TO DO

1. Make Praising Cards.
   a. Copy cards from this chapter.
   b. Read and talk about the following verses. Use a dictionary if you need help. You could copy the verses or rewrite them in your own words.
      • 1 Chronicles 29:10-13
      • Jeremiah 32:17
2. Use a hymn book to help you find ideas for Praising Cards.

THANKING

Chapter 6

THANKS FOR FISH AND FUN AND FEELINGS

Ryan had been so busy the first week at the ranch that there wasn't time to be lonely. But this morning, when he thought about Mom and Dad, Meghan and Jason, his stomach hurt.

Today was his birthday, the first one away from home. Of course, there would be no celebration. He couldn't expect Uncle Grady and Aunt Marta to remember.

Ryan thought about something his mother often said: "Activity is the best medicine for loneliness." He jumped out of bed.

I'd better take a super dose of activity today, Ryan thought.

At breakfast, his aunt and uncle were their cheerful selves, but no one mentioned Ryan's birthday.

47

"Would you like to run an errand with me?" Uncle Grady asked.

"Sure," said Ryan, trying to sound excited.

"I'd like to go, too," Aunt Marta said, putting on her tan camping hat and her sunglasses.

The Jeep was loaded with a basket and a long box. Ryan didn't really notice. He climbed into the back seat, pushing them aside.

Stately ponderosa pines lined the gravel road. Deer grazed in the open meadows, and beyond them the tallest mountains were still blanketed with snow.

As they neared Williams Creek campground, Marta said, "Oh, Grady, please drive down by the lake. I love to see the ducks in the morning."

At the shore they stood quietly and watched the ducks maneuver. When the ducks dipped their heads in search of food, their fuzzy white tails went up in the air.

What a spectacular sight—the ducks, the lake, and the snow-covered mountains. Ryan remembered Aunt Marta's Praising Card from Psalm 95: "The mountain peaks belong to God. The sea is His, for He made it."

"Surprise!"

Out from behind five trees jumped five kids from the Sunday school class: Kevin, his twin sister Kristin, Holly, Josh, and Danny.

"Happy birthday!" They shouted in unison.

From the Jeep, Uncle Grady took out the long package. "Here, Ryan. Better open this now. You'll need it."

Ryan ripped off the brown wrapping paper. "Wow! A fishing rod and reel."

"Here's something from all of us," said Kevin.

"Imitation flies!" Ryan exclaimed. "They look real. I can fool rainbow trout with these."

"It takes a little skill too," said Kristin. Her sparkling eyes challenged him. She pulled her long brown hair up and tied it into a ponytail.

49

With pant legs rolled up, six barefoot kids lined the sandy shore. Fishing lines looped back and forth as the kids cast the flies out on the lake, reeled them in, and cast again. Ryan tried to copy their actions. *It's not easy,* he thought, untangling his line from a bush.

Not a word was spoken, except for the cheers when someone landed a trout. And that was usually Kristin.

When the sun was high overhead, Uncle Grady announced, "It's time to clean those trout for lunch. You all know the rule: you catch it, you clean it."

"You gotta be kiddin'!" Danny Hathaway tossed his trout at Uncle Grady's feet. "That's a stupid rule."

Danny was small for a twelve-year-old, and his short bristly hair was greasy-looking. His eyes were defiant; his lips, pouty. People didn't trust him. Even his grandmother called him Devious Dan.

Uncle Grady looked at Aunt Marta and shrugged his shoulders.

Ryan watched the other kids clean their fish while Uncle Grady built a fire. Soon the trout were sizzling over glowing coals.

Holly's mother had driven the kids to the lake. Now she and Aunt Marta spread out the picnic lunch—fresh grilled trout, potato salad, Western baked beans with homemade bread—and for dessert, a gooey three-layer chocolate cake.

After lunch, Ryan said, "Thanks, everyone, for the

gifts and the birthday picnic."

Uncle Grady patted his full stomach. "Now, we need some exercise. Let's hike around the lake."

When the group returned, the sun was sinking behind the mountains. Everyone waved goodbye and headed home.

At the dinner table, Aunt Marta said, "I have a present for you too."

Opening the box, Ryan found a brown leather Bible.

"This is my first Bible," Ryan said. "Thanks. This is the best birthday I've ever had."

"There's Someone else we should thank," suggested Aunt Marta. Looking at Uncle Grady, she said, "You begin. When you finish, Ryan and I will thank God for something."

Uncle Grady began, "O God, You are the great Creator. Your world is wonderful. Thanks for allowing us to enjoy it today."

Aunt Marta continued. "Dear Heavenly Father, we know You care about us and want us to have joy. Thank You for Your great love and for this day of fun and play."

Ryan added, "Thanks, Lord, for the ducks on the lake, the fish we ate, and the lonesome feelings You took away."

Uncle Grady said, "Amen."

Aunt Marta's hands were still folded in prayer.

She held up her index finger. "Ryan, can you guess what the second ingredient of prayer is?"

"It's got to be saying thanks," he said. "That one will be easy for me to remember. I'll just think of my eleventh birthday."

TO THINK ABOUT
You are my God, and I will give you thanks;
you are my God, and I will exalt you.
(Psalm 118:28)

TO TALK ABOUT
1. a. In the verse above, what two things does the writer promise to do?
   b. What does exalt mean?
2. In their prayers, Uncle Grady and Aunt Marta used the first two ingredients of prayer.
   a. What are their praising lines?
   b. What are their thanking lines?
3. What things did Ryan, Aunt Marta, and Uncle Grady thank God for?

TO DO
1. Use these verses to make Thanking Cards:
   • Psalm 40:5
   • Psalm 107:8-9
2. Make a Thanking Card by completing this sentence:

THANKING

I'm thankful for the seasons
You made, O God, especially
—————— since I enjoy

——————————— .

Chapter 7

THANKS FOR RAINY DAYS TOO

A few days later, during breakfast, the wind blew fiercely. Driving rain filled every ditch and gully.

Ryan pressed his nose against the living room window. He couldn't even see the barn. *Sure can't go riding in this rain,* he thought. *What a bummer this day is going to be!*

"What are you thinking about?" asked Uncle Grady.

"The rain! Our plans are ruined. How can we have fun on a dreary day like this?"

"I guess your aunt and I will have to show you how we spend a rainy day. Maybe you'll like it."

"I never liked rainy days at home. So why should it be any different here?"

"You'll see. First, let's build a fire."

55

On the brick hearth, Uncle Grady shaved thin strips of wood from dry logs. He heaped this tinder on a newspaper and laid it in the fireplace. On top of the tinder, he carefully arranged small sticks in the shape of an Indian tepee. Around them, he placed split logs. Minutes after he lit it the fire was blazing.

"I feel better already," said Ryan.

"Fire can be a friend," said Uncle Grady. "It brightens the darkness, warms the body, and chases away the gloomies."

"So does music," added Aunt Marta, putting a tape in the recorder. Folding the lace tablecloth, she said to Ryan, "See that stack of puzzles on the corner shelf? Pick out one that interests you."

Ryan returned with a 500-piece jigsaw puzzle of an Indian chief in full headdress. "This looks interesting."

"And hard." Aunt Marta laughed, pushing her hair behind her ears. "We'll be busy all day. Dump out the pieces."

Ryan helped his aunt turn each piece right side up and group them by color.

Uncle Grady pulled up a chair. "I'll work on the border."

For an hour the three concentrated on the Indian chief, whose feathered headdress proved to be quite a challenge.

"Working on a puzzle with you guys is fun," said

Ryan, interrupting the silence.

"Togetherness is always fun." Marta stretched, and rubbed her eyes. "Let's do something else. We can come back anytime and put in more pieces."

"I think I'll bake some oatmeal cookies." Uncle Grady headed for the kitchen. "Anybody want to help?"

"You're going to bake?" Ryan asked in surprise. "That's a woman's job!"

"Who do you think does the cooking when all the cowboys go on a three-day roundup?" asked Uncle Grady.

"H-m-m, never thought of that," Ryan said.

"Come and help. You'll see how much fun it can be to create something out of a list of ingredients."

"How can I help?" asked Ryan.

"You run the mixer. I'll gather the ingredients," said Uncle Grady. "Marta, would you chop the nuts?"

Two glasses of milk and four oatmeal cookies later, Ryan admitted it had been fun and certainly worth the effort.

"Let's take time out for a little Bible study," suggested Uncle Grady.

When Ryan returned with his new Bible, Aunt Marta and Uncle Grady were seated at the old oak table.

"What are we going to study today?" asked Ryan.

"Thanking God," said Aunt Marta. "A good key

verse is Psalm 105:1. Let's look at it."

After everyone found the place, Uncle Grady read: "Give thanks to the LORD, call on his name; make known among the nations what he has done."

Aunt Marta explained, "We call this our *key* for making Thanking Cards, because it tells us to thank God for what He has done."

"We can thank God for what He has done in the past—things recorded in the Bible," said Uncle Grady. "Or we can thank Him for what He is doing for us today."

"Psalm 136 is a good thanking psalm," Aunt Marta said as she passed out the cards and pencils. Then she began writing:

THANKING

Thank You, Lord, for Your mighty miracle when You parted the Red Sea. You saved Your people but drowned the Egyptians. Your miracles remind me that Your love lasts forever.

Psalm 136:13-15

"I know one," Ryan said.

> **THANKING**
> Thank You, God, for helping
> David kill the lion and bear
> when they attacked his sheep.
> Thanks for protecting the lambs
> and for watching over me, too.

"First Thessalonians 5:18 says, 'Give thanks in all circumstances.' Has anything happened that you thought you couldn't be thankful for?" asked Marta.

"I wasn't thankful for this rainy day." Ryan wrote:

> **THANKING**
> Thank You, Lord, for this vacation.
> I even want to thank You for
> this rainy day and for teaching me
> how much fun a family can have
> doing things together.

TO THINK ABOUT

Always giving thanks to God the Father for every-thing, in the name of our Lord Jesus Christ.
(Ephesians 5:20)

TO TALK ABOUT

1. Ephesians 5:20 says to give thanks for everything. Talk about things to thank God for that you have taken for granted in the past.
2. In 1 Thessalonians 5:18, Paul said we should give thanks in all situations.
   a. What experiences have you had that were unpleasant?
   b. Think of something to thank God for in spite of the unhappy situation.

TO DO

1. Make Thanking Cards for some of the things you talked about.
2. You can also choose from the following Bible verses to make Thanking Cards.
   • Acts 14:17
   • Ephesians 2:4-5
   • James 1:17
   • 1 John 3:1

Chapter 8

COCKLEBURS AND CURRYCOMBS

"Do you go on these rides often?" Ryan asked, wiping the sweat from Rustler's back.

"At least once a week," Aunt Marta replied. "It's my date with Grady and Prince." She tied her gentle Appaloosa to the corral fence and took off the saddle.

Uncle Grady brought out the basket of grooming tools. "Before and after every ride we groom the horses."

"Ouch!" Aunt Marta exclaimed. "Just look at these cockleburs Prince picked up on the trail." Carefully she combed through his tail.

"Grooming helps keep horses healthy," Uncle Grady said, pulling the rubber currycomb through the dried mud on King's legs. He took a hoof pick from the basket. "You watch now, and I'll show you how to remove dirt and stones from Rustler's hoof."

When they finished grooming the horses, Ryan stroked Rustler's forehead. Rustler nickered and pushed his muzzle into Ryan's chest.

"I think he's saying thanks," said Ryan.

"Horses have good memories, you know," said Uncle Grady. "Rustler won't forget your grooming."

Walking past Ryan, Aunt Marta gave him her usual pat on the cheek. "If I don't want you to forget my good cooking, I'd better head for the kitchen."

"And Ryan and I are heading for the barn to clean the stalls," Uncle Grady said.

Dragging his feet in the dust, Ryan followed his uncle. "I didn't know owning horses was so much work."

"With every pleasure comes responsibility," Uncle Grady said, handing Ryan a pitchfork. "You can clean Rustler's stall. Load the wet straw into the wheelbarrow."

"Yuk! What a stinky job."

"You can't have horses without manure," said Uncle Grady, slapping Ryan on the back. "When you're through, I'll show you where to dump the wheelbarrow."

After Rustler's stall was clean, Ryan spread fresh pine shavings on the floor. Carefully, he measured the grain and poured it into the manger. Then he filled the wooden rack with hay.

When Ryan finished the job, he climbed up on the corral fence and watched his uncle shoeing King, the palomino.

"The Rocky Mountains are hard on horseshoes," Uncle Grady said, taking another nail out of his leather apron.

"I like King's golden coat and his silvery mane and tail," Ryan said. "I like his smooth muscles, too. Is he the horse you ride in the rodeos?"

That was all Uncle Grady needed to start him talking about his favorite subjects—horses and rodeos. His stories were funny and exciting. Listening to him was better than watching TV.

Before long the clanging cowbell called them to dinner.

At the table, Ryan excitedly talked with his mouth full. "This is de-lish! I've never eaten this before. What is it?"

"It's my chicken and dumplings."

Ryan wiped gravy from his chin with a red checkered napkin. "It's good. You're a great cook!"

Aunt Marta's smile spread from ear to ear. "You're learning how to give both praise and thanksgiving."

"What's the difference between praise and thanksgiving?" Ryan asked. "It seems to me they sort of run together."

"You're right." Aunt Marta handed a bowl of cherry cobbler to Ryan. "Praise is saying something

63

good about God, His worth or His works. Thankfulness is expressing appreciation for those things when they affect you."

"Here's an example," said Uncle Grady. "If I say, 'God is a wonderful and wise Creator,' that would be praising God. But, if I say, 'Thank You, God, for making horses, because they're so much fun to ride,' that would be giving thanks."

"Tonight, I'm going to make some Thanking Cards," Ryan said, "for people like Pastor Olson, my Colorado friends, and my aunt and uncle."

After Ryan made four Thanking Cards, he put them in one pile. Beside them he stacked his Praising Cards. "Are we going to make cards for all five parts of prayer?" he asked.

"That's my plan," said Aunt Marta.

"How can I tell the cards apart?"

"Try these." Aunt Marta laid her colored markers on the table.

Ryan colored a purple border around his Praising Cards. He put a blue one around his Thanking Cards.

"You could draw something on the cards," Uncle Grady suggested, looking up from the *Western Horseman* magazine he was reading.

"Good idea," said Ryan. "Since God is King of the entire world, I'll draw a crown on the Praising Cards."

"What will you draw on your Thanking Cards?" Aunt Marta asked.

"A smiling face," answered Ryan, "because being thankful makes me happy."

"Thinking thankful thoughts makes humans as happy as. . . ." Uncle Grady frowned and scratched his head.

Ryan repeated, "Thinking thankful thoughts makes humans as happy as good grooming does horses."

Uncle Grady nodded and winked.

"You've got to work on that wink, Uncle Grady. Watch this."

Ryan winked slowly, slyly, and smoothly. "See! No scrunches, no wrinkles, no wiggles. Now you try it."

"Like you said, I'll work on it." Uncle Grady grinned and went back to reading his magazine.

TO THINK ABOUT
I thank my God every time I remember you. In all my prayers for all of you, I always pray with joy because of your partnership in the gospel.
(Philippians 1:3-5)

TO TALK ABOUT
1. a. In the verses above, who did the Apostle Paul thank God for?
   b. How often?
   c. With what kind of attitude?
2. Plutarch, a Greek philosopher, said, "The worship

most acceptable to God comes from a thankful and cheerful heart." Do you think this is true? Why?

3. Uncle Grady believes thankful people are happy people. Think about people you know. Is this true?

4. Uncle Grady said, "You can't have horses without manure." Can you change that to fit something in your life? Example: You can't play the piano without. . . .

TO DO

1. Make Thanking Cards for special people in your life. Tell why you are grateful for each one.

2. Choose colored markers or crayons to code your cards so you can easily recognize the Praising Cards and Thanking Cards. You can color a border and draw a simple picture in one corner of each card, as Ryan did.

CONFESSING

Chapter 9

BREAKING
RANCH RULES

"We don't let a little thing like that ruin our day," Ryan said, snugging up the cinch on Rustler's saddle. "I learned that lesson last week."

Stepping into the stirrup and mounting Rustler, he continued his one-sided conversation.

"So, it's just you and me. Uncle Grady and Aunt Marta went shopping in Pagosa Springs. Kevin and Kristin can't ride today, so I'll have to stay on the ranch. But that's okay. I need lots of practice."

Ryan rode Rustler around the corral. They walked, they jogged, they loped.

"Good boy, Rustler!" Ryan patted him on the neck.

Next, Ryan placed the yellow barrels exactly where Kristin had showed him. The quarter horse raced around the barrels in a three-leaf clover pattern.

Whenever he knocked a barrel over, Ryan dismounted and set it up again.

Wish Kristin was here, he thought. *This gets to be work when you're riding alone.*

Ryan led Rustler to the watering tank. "It's hot and dusty in that corral. Drink up, boy."

Soaking his neckerchief in the horse tank, Ryan wiped his own face and neck. "Let's do something exciting. Let's go exploring."

A voice inside Ryan's head spoke: *You know the ranch rule—Never go riding in the San Juan Forest alone.*

Ryan argued, "I won't get lost. Besides, I'm not going far. Uncle Grady will never know I left the ranch."

Across the western pasture they loped. At the gate, Ryan slid out of the saddle, opened the gate, and led Rustler through. Then he closed and latched the gate.

"See, there," Ryan said aloud, trying to quiet the tiny voice inside him. "I obeyed the second rule: 'Always close every gate you pass through.'"

It was cooler in the forest beneath the evergreens. Ryan rode with confidence. After all, he had been in these woods before. He knew how to watch his trail. What else did he need to know?

When they came to an alpine park, Ryan dismounted. It felt good to stretch his legs. He pulled off his boots and socks and put his sweaty feet into the icy stream. Rustler chomped on the thick grass.

Lying down beside the stream, Ryan picked a long weed and stuck it between the gap in his front teeth. He wiggled his toes in the sun. *I feel like Tom Sawyer*, he thought.

"*Wheck-wek-wek-wek-wek!*" From high in the nearby aspen trees, a Steller's jay scolded him for invading its privacy.

The sounds of nature were very different from the sounds of the city. He closed his eyes and listened. Fluttering aspen leaves rattled in the breeze, water splashed over boulders, and insects hummed in the wild daisies near his head.

When Ryan opened his eyes, the sun was touching the western peaks. *I must have been tired from all that riding*, he thought, as he sat up and pulled on his boots.

He led Rustler to a fallen tree. Standing on the tree, he stepped easily into the stirrup and swung the other leg over the saddle.

In the forest, the late sun made long shadows of the tall pine trees. Bushes and boulders looked different now. After riding for half an hour, Ryan pulled on the reins.

"Whoa, Rustler. I don't recognize anything. I think I'm lost."

Ryan's confidence disappeared as quickly as a

prairie dog goes down its hole.

Rustler whinnied and pawed the ground.

"You want to go home, boy? So do I. But I don't know which way to go."

Rustler jerked his head forward, pulling on the reins.

"That's it," Ryan said aloud, remembering what Pete had told him: "'If you're ever lost, let the reins go slack. Give the horse his head. He knows the way home.'"

With both legs Ryan squeezed the horse. "Go, Rustler. Go home."

When they came out of the forest, Ryan stroked Rustler's neck. "Good job, old boy."

Before him lay the ranch. The cows were feeding in the pasture. Beyond them was the barn. He could even see the hairpin curves on the gravel road that led to town. Rounding one curve was a pickup. Behind it was a green Jeep.

"Oh, no! Here comes Uncle Grady," Ryan exclaimed.

Ryan slapped Rustler's rump with the tips of the reins. They galloped to the western pasture. Ryan slid down, opened the gate, struggled back into the saddle, and raced for the barn.

Inside the corral, Ryan jerked off the saddle. With a soft cloth he wiped the sweat off Rustler's shiny coat. He saw the Jeep stop at the corral gate.

"Where are the Bennett twins?" Grady called out.

"Kevin phoned right after you left. Said they had to help their dad. I've been practicing in the corral all day."

The little voice inside him whispered, *That's a lie.*

Uncle Grady chuckled. "You'll be a better cowboy than I am if you practice that much every day. How about helping me unload the Jeep?"

After Ryan carried in the groceries, he returned to the corral. He led Rustler to his stall and put away the saddle and bridle."

You disobeyed. You lied, said the nagging voice.

Ryan kicked the stall door. "Shut up!" he shouted. "I didn't get hurt, and I didn't get lost. Uncle Grady will never know. So just shut up!"

TO THINK ABOUT
Even a child is known by his actions, by whether his conduct is pure and right. (Proverbs 20:11)

TO TALK ABOUT
1. *Character* is what you think and feel on the inside that affects how you talk and act on the outside.

   Reputation is what other people think about you, by watching what you do and listening to what you say.

   a. Which part of Proverbs 20:11 is talking about reputation?

   b. Which part is about character?

2. a. How can disobeying and lying affect your character?

   b. How can it affect your reputation?

3. a. How did one sin lead to another for Ryan?

   b. What do you think he will do next?

TO DO

This would be a good time to finish coloring and coding your Praising and Thanking Cards before you begin the third group.

Chapter 10

LOST IN THE MOUNTAINS

"Fixing fences is hard work," said Ryan, digging out a broken fence post.

"But very important." Uncle Grady stretched new barbed wire between the posts. "A broken fence means trouble. If cows get into the young alfalfa fields, they could ruin the entire crop. If they go into the national forest, they could break a leg or get lost."

Ryan and his uncle put the pick and shovel in the Jeep, climbed in, and drove slowly along the fence line.

"When do we eat?" asked Ryan. "I'm hungry."

"You're always hungry." His uncle laughed. "Pete has our lunch with him. He and Jake, another cowhand, are fixing the south fence. We'll meet at the west gate at noon."

When they finally neared the west gate, Uncle

Grady frowned. "We have troubles. Jump out and close that gate, Ryan."

Ryan bounded out of the Jeep. While he was closing the gate, he recalled yesterday when he went riding alone. He remembered how he was sitting on the other side of the fence enjoying the view when he saw the green Jeep heading for the ranch.

Oh no! he thought. *I left the gate open.* He trudged back to the Jeep. *If I tell Uncle Grady I left the gate open, he'll know I broke his ranch rule and went riding alone in the forest.*

"I wonder how long that gate's been open. Do you know anything about it, Ryan?"

"Nope! Might have been Pete or Jake."

"Old cowhands? Not likely."

"Maybe—maybe it was a careless hiker."

When Pete and Jake arrived, everyone ate chicken salad sandwiches, apples, and brownies.

"Well, Pete, we've got a big job ahead of us," said Uncle Grady.

"Harder than fixing fences?"

"This west gate was open. I'm sure we've got some stray cows out there."

"That's strange." Pete drained his coffee cup. "The gate was closed on Monday when I was counting broken posts."

"The important thing now is to find out how many cattle are missing," Uncle Grady said. "You and

Jake count the cows in the east pasture. I'll check this pasture, and we'll meet at the corral."

An hour later, Pete announced, "Altogether, four cows and a calf are missing."

Ryan's stomach felt as if it were full of tumbling sagebrush. What if they couldn't find them? How could he pay for the lost cattle?

Everyone saddled a horse, including Aunt Marta. Keeping in view of each other, they rode up and down the canyons, through streams, and over one ridge after another.

No wonder Uncle Grady has ranch rules, thought Ryan, ducking his head to miss a low pine branch.

Late in the afternoon, Jake found three cows in a grassy park.

"That's it for tonight," called out Uncle Grady. "We can't search in the dark. Let's herd these three back to the ranch."

All night Ryan twisted and turned in his bed, tugging on his blanket. *It's all my fault,* he thought. *I've sure caused a lot of trouble. Where could the missing cow and her calf be? What if something terrible happens to them?*

His anxious mind made up weird stories. *What if they fall off a cliff, or break a leg? What if they're attacked by wolves, or stolen by outlaws? What if . . . ?*

Ryan hardly slept all night.

77

TO THINK ABOUT

Obey your leaders and submit to their authority.
They keep watch over you as men who must give
an account. Obey them so that their work will be a
joy, not a burden. (Hebrews 13:17)

TO TALK ABOUT

1. Hebrews 13:17 is for everybody: grandparents,
   parents, and children. Name some leaders you
   should obey. Think of your home, school, church,
   clubs, community, country.
2. There's usually a reason for every rule, but you may
   not understand it. Talk about rules from home,
   school, or work. Then think of reasons for them.
3. How did Ryan's disobedience become a burden for
   Uncle Grady?
4. a. How can obeying your leaders bring them joy?
   b. How can disobeying them be a burden?

TO DO

When you memorize Bible verses, you are helping to
build a good character. These thoughts will come to
your mind and help you make important decisions.

Every family member could copy Hebrews 13:17
on a 3″ x 5″ card. Now tape the cards to prominent
places, like the refrigerator door or the bathroom
mirror. It can be fun to memorize Scripture as a
family.

78

Chapter 11

A COW, A CALF, AND A NAGGING CONSCIENCE

Early in the morning the five riders began searching again. Today the ridges got higher and the canyons got deeper. Scrub oak tore at Ryan's jeans as Rustler walked through thick brush.

Going down a steep slope, the horse stumbled on loose rocks and fell on his front knees.

"Help!" screamed Ryan, grabbing Rustler's neck. He slid forward and landed under Rustler's nose.

This is not fun, he thought as he brushed off the dirt, picked up his hat, and climbed back into the saddle. *This is work—hard and dangerous work.*

And you know why, the nagging voice whispered. *You disobeyed, and you've told two lies. How many more will you tell to hide the truth?*

Ryan wiped his sweaty forehead on his sleeve.

On the top of Echo Ridge, Ryan heard Pete hollering, "Over here! Over here! I've found them!"

The calf was caught in a thicket. Its mother was standing nearby, bawling.

Pete tied a rope around the cow and led her away while Uncle Grady untangled the calf's hind leg from the thorny branches.

Thirty minutes later, everyone was headed for the ranch, including the cow and her limping calf.

At the corral, Aunt Marta said, "If someone will take care of Prince, I'll fix something to eat."

The men unsaddled the horses and brushed them down.

"Uncle Grady, I have something to tell you." Ryan stuttered, "I—I disobeyed you, and—and then I lied." He told the whole story, right there in the barn. "I'm sorry. Will you guys forgive me?"

"You're forgiven," Pete said. He tipped his hat and left the barn.

"I'm glad you told us," Uncle Grady said as he hung the bridles on their hooks. "Do you think there is Someone else you should ask forgiveness of?"

"You mean God," Ryan said.

"That's right."

"I guess I could do that tonight before I go to bed."

"What's wrong with right now?"

Ryan looked around at the horses and the hay. "Here? In the barn?"

"Sure, God is always listening. We can talk to Him any place, anytime."

They knelt together in an empty stall. Ryan felt tears smarting in his eyes. He told God he was sorry for breaking the ranch rules, but more than that, for breaking God's rules.

After dinner, Aunt Marta said to Ryan, "For having put in such a hard day, you look happy tonight."

He told her the whole story. "For two days, I felt like a tractor was on my chest, but tonight I feel good."

"Confessing your sins to God always replaces heaviness with happiness," she said.

Uncle Grady placed the woodcarving of the praying hands on the table. "Tonight is a good time to talk about the third ingredient of prayer."

"It must have something to do with getting into trouble, because I sure did plenty of that," Ryan said.

"It's about getting out of trouble," Aunt Marta said. She smiled and picked up the woodcarving. "The longest finger of the folded hands will remind you that the third ingredient of prayer is confessing your sins to God."

"At first, that was hard," Ryan said. "I was afraid to say I told a lie. But once I started to confess, it got easier."

"God is waiting to forgive us," said Uncle Grady. "Jesus already paid the price for our sins when He gave His life on the cross. All we have to do is confess

81

our sins to God and believe that He hears and forgives."

"Would you like to make some Confessing Cards?" Aunt Marta asked. "This is usually the most difficult part of prayer. No one likes to admit he's done something wrong. But Confessing Cards help us."

"I need all the help I can get," Ryan admitted. "This isn't as much fun as making Praising and Thanking Cards, but I know what to write on my first card."

CONFESSING

Dear God, I'm sorry I disobeyed Uncle Grady and that I caused him so much trouble. And please forgive me for the lies I told, too.

"That's good," said Uncle Grady. "Always be specific when you confess your sins to God. Name each one instead of saying, 'Forgive me if I did or said anything I shouldn't have.' Admitting what you did wrong will make you strong."

"I've got an idea," said Aunt Marta. "You can make

several fill-in-the-blank cards. Then you can use the same cards whenever that little voice reminds you of something you need to confess."

Aunt Marta made these two cards for Ryan.

CONFESSING
I confess that I lied to _____
_____ when I said __
_____.
Please forgive me, God, for lying.

CONFESSING
I confess that I disobeyed _____
_____ when I _____
_____. I'm
sorry, Lord. Please forgive me
for doing wrong.

Ryan took out his red marker. "I'm going to put a red border on these Confessing Cards because the blood of Jesus takes away my sins. And I'll draw a heart in the corner to remind me how God took away the heaviness and made me happy again."

TO TALK ABOUT

If we confess our sins, he is faithful and just and will forgive us our sins and purify us from all unrighteousness. (1 John 1:9)

TO THINK ABOUT

1. What is the first word in the verse above? God's forgiveness depends on an action from us. We must take the first step and confess our sins to Him.
2. Someone might ask, "How will I know when I have sinned?" Everyone has a little voice inside him like Ryan had, or a funny feeling that tells you when you do a wrong thing. Some people call it your conscience. Tell about times when that little voice told you that you weren't doing what you should.

TO DO

1. Make Confessing Cards, as Ryan and Marta did. Choose your border color and symbol.
2. Make a Confessing Card like the one on the following page.

CONFESSING
I want to confess my wrong
_____ (actions, words,
or attitudes). I'm sorry, Lord.
Please forgive me for _____
(tell exactly what you did, said,
or felt).

3. Do you have some sins you want to confess now?
God is ready to hear you anytime or anywhere. You
can use one of the cards you just made to help you.

ASKING FOR OTHERS

Chapter 12

RODEO RIDERS

It was the Fourth of July. Firecrackers whistled. Flags fluttered in the breeze. The aroma of hot buttered popcorn filled the air.

Someone shouted, "Program. Get your souvenir program. Only two dollars."

A vendor yelled, "Ice-cold Coke. Ice-cold Coke."

Ryan and Aunt Marta moved with the flow of people gathering in the arena. They climbed to the sixth row of the bleachers and sat down on the splintery planks.

"I've never been to a rodeo before," Ryan said, as the band started playing.

The wide gate at the south end of the arena swung open. In came the first rider, carrying the American flag. Following him were sixty horses, with riders in colorful shirts, big hats, and leather chaps. They paraded around the arena, welcoming everyone to the Red Ryder Roundup.

"There's Uncle Grady and Pete," said Aunt Marta.

"Good luck," shouted Ryan, waving as they rode by. "I wish I was good enough to ride in a rodeo."

"You will be, if you keep practicing. Pete and your uncle rode in their first rodeos when they were teenagers. And they've been riding ever since."

"Do they always win?" Ryan asked.

"Oh my, no. No one wins all the time. But they like being part of the excitement."

The master of ceremonies announced, "The first event this afternoon is the wild horse race. Are you ready?"

The crowd hooted and hollered.

Ryan laughed and cheered as teams of three men each tried to saddle, mount, and ride wild horses. No one succeeded, but that didn't seem to matter.

The second event was the calf-roping contest. Ryan watched five riders compete for the best time.

"Pete is next," said Aunt Marta.

"Is he good?"

"You'll see."

The announcer said, "The next contestant is a world champion. Let's see if Pete O'Neill can beat his own record."

"Champion!" Ryan gasped. "He never told me."

"Pete wouldn't. He never brags about anything. He's a great cowhand—good at everything he does."

The gate opened. The calf shot out of the chute. Swinging his lariat, Pete rode alongside the calf and sent the loop sailing through the air. It landed around the calf's neck.

Instantly, Pete's horse stopped, keeping the rope tight. Pete dismounted, ran to the calf, and threw it to the ground. Quicker than lightning flashes, he tied three of the calf's feet with a piggin' string. He pushed his hands high above his head, signaling the end of his run.

Ryan jumped up. Beating the air with his fists, he shouted, "Yeah, Pete! Yeah, Pete!"

"He did it!" bellowed the announcer above the noise of the stomping, cheering crowd. "Pete O'Neill has set a new record."

The steer-wrestling contest was next, and Uncle Grady was the second contestant. He rode at top speed alongside a steer, leaped for its horns, and tried to throw it to the ground. He must have drawn a strong and stubborn steer, because he couldn't pull it down before the buzzer sounded.

"How about a Coke and some popcorn?" asked Aunt Marta. "That makes losing less painful." She motioned to a man, carrying a tray of drinks and bags of popcorn.

Pete and Uncle Grady paired up for the team roping contest. They came out of the chutes, swinging their lariats and chasing a steer. Pete's loop fell over the steer's horns. Uncle Grady's loop caught its hind legs.

Perfect! Ryan thought.

Almost. They finished in second place.

"Hang on to your seats!" the announcer shouted. "We've got the meanest horses in the West for this next event, the saddle-bronc riding. The cowboy must leave the starting gate with both feet in the stirrups and both spurs against the horse's shoulders. He must keep one hand in the air for eight seconds."

"Your uncle loves this event, but I really wish he wouldn't ride in it. He's not as young as he used to be, and it seems like the horses get meaner every year."

Ryan watched the first cowboy get bucked off before the buzzer sounded. Daring clowns distracted the wild horse while the rider limped away.

The second cowboy stayed on until the pickup men pulled him out of the saddle.

"The third bronco buster is Grady Simpson," shouted the announcer. "He's a native of Colorado, and he's been riding since he was fifteen. Today he's on the meanest bronco of all—Crashing Thunder. This one's a real killer. Hang in there, Grady."

The gate opened. Crashing Thunder came out bucking! He jumped! He kicked! He turned in circles while Uncle Grady waved one hand high in the air.

92

Ryan held his breath until the buzzer finally sounded. "What a great ride! He ought to get a high score for that."

But the bronco wouldn't stop bucking and turning. The pickup men couldn't get close enough to help Uncle Grady off. With one ferocious kick, Crashing Thunder threw its rider.

Uncle Grady went flying through the air, banging against the heavy wooden gates that encircled the arena. With his face in the dirt, Uncle Grady lay still.

Ryan cringed and sucked in his breath. He grabbed

93

his aunt's arm. "I'm scared, Aunt Marta."
"So am I, Ryan," she whispered. "So am I."

TO THINK ABOUT

For I am the LORD, your God,
  who takes hold of your right hand
and says to you, Do not fear;
  I will help you.   (Isaiah 41:13)

TO TALK ABOUT

1. Think of times when you were afraid—like during
   a storm, a test at school, an accident, a serious
   illness. Talk about how you felt.
2. a. In the verse above, who promises to help us?
   b. How close is He?
3. a. Ryan had a dream to ride in a rodeo someday.
      How can he make that dream come true?
   b. What are some of your dreams or goals?
   c. How can you make them happen?

TO DO

Memorize Isaiah 41:13. (Younger children can memorize Psalm 56:3.) The next time you're afraid, you
can recall this verse and know that God will keep His
promise.

Chapter 13

BECOMING A GO-BETWEEN

A doctor wearing a blue mask and gown entered the emergency waiting room. He walked over to Aunt Marta. "Mrs. Simpson? I'm Dr. Meadows. I'm sorry it's taken so long. Your husband had quite an accident. He has a broken leg and a serious head injury. I can fix his leg." He paused. "I'm not sure about his head."

Ryan didn't hear any more of the conversation. He couldn't imagine the ranch without Uncle Grady.

A tap on the shoulder startled him. "I'm going back to the rodeo arena," said Pete, "to pick up our horses. I'm leaving you in charge of your aunt."

Aunt Marta was sitting on a sofa reading her small New Testament.

Ryan sat beside her. "What will we do, Aunt Marta?"

"We'll pray. God is sovereign. He's in control of everything."

"You mean, God made this accident happen?"

"Oh, no. I don't believe God made it happen, but I do believe that God is in charge of the results. It's my job to pray and trust. It's God's job to direct the outcome."

She slipped her hand over Ryan's and prayed softly: "O sovereign God, You are in charge of all nature, all nations, and all people. You are in charge of Grady just now. You made his body, so You understand the injury in his head. The doctors don't know if he will recover. But I know You are a miracle-working God—the same yesterday, today, and forever. Please make Grady well. I know You can, if it fits in with Your great plan. Because You are good and everything You do is right, O God, I trust Grady into Your hands. Give Ryan and me peace and strength to get through this night. In Jesus' name. Amen."

"I've never heard anyone pray like that before," Ryan said softly.

Aunt Marta wiped the tears from her eyes. "When we pray for others, we call it interceding. I love that word. *Inter* means between; *cede* means to go. So intercessory praying means you *go between*. You go between God and someone in need. I went between Grady and God, asking for healing. That's the fourth ingredient of prayer. Usually I call it *asking help for* others. That's easier to remember than *interceding*."

A nurse carrying pillows and blankets came into the room. "Still no change. Your husband hasn't regained consciousness yet. We don't know what else to do for him."

"It's all right. God knows. We're trusting Him to take care of Grady," Aunt Marta said.

The nurse shrugged her shoulders and laid down the bedding. "Make yourselves comfortable."

Ryan stretched out on the brown sofa. "She doesn't know God the way you do, does she?"

"Perhaps not." Aunt Marta covered her knees with a blanket. "But someday, when she needs Him, she'll remember tonight."

Ryan prayed silently: "Dear God, I'm scared. Is it all right to tell You that? We really need You tonight. The doctors and nurses can't help Uncle Grady. There's no one left, except You. Please make him well. And help Aunt Marta. She seems strong, but I think she's worried too."

The waiting room wasn't the quietest place to sleep. Nurses scurried up and down the hall. Lights shone in Ryan's face. The sofa was hard. Every time Ryan opened his eyes, he saw his aunt praying or reading her New Testament.

In the morning they went to the cafeteria. Aunt Marta drank black coffee and nibbled on a piece of whole wheat toast. Ryan took only a few bites of the scrambled eggs and crisp bacon.

When they returned to the waiting room, Dr. Meadows was standing in the doorway. "I can't understand what has happened, Mrs. Simpson," he said. "Grady is awake and joking with the nurses. He's asking to see you both. Don't stay too long." He disappeared down the hall.

Ryan squeezed his aunt's hand. "We know what happened, don't we? You go first. I'll phone Pete and tell him the good news."

TO THINK ABOUT
Pray for each other so that you may be healed. The prayer of a righteous man is powerful and effective. (James 5:16)

TO TALK ABOUT
1. a. How did Aunt Marta define intercessory prayer?
   b. In James 5:16, what are four words that mean "to intercede"?
2. a. According to James 5:16, whose prayers will be answered?
   b. Do you believe Aunt Marta is a righteous woman? Why?
3. When Ryan prayed, he was a go-between for two people. Who were they and what were their needs?
4. God's power is like the water behind a dam, waiting to be released. How can you release it?

TO DO

1. Make a list of family members or friends who need a go-between because of sickness, an accident, or some other trouble.

2. Make Asking for Others Cards. Here's an example:

ASKING FOR OTHERS
God please help Natalie just now. You know all about her sickness and pain. You made our bodies, Lord. You have the power to heal. Please make her well.

---

3. Ryan decided to draw a foot in a cast on his Asking for Others Cards. Choose a symbol and border color for your cards.

Chapter 14

SECRETS AROUND A CAMPFIRE

Uncle Grady was back at the ranch, sitting on the redwood recliner reading a Western novel. The white plaster cast, autographed daily by Ryan, was propped up on pillows.

"I've finished cleaning the stalls," Ryan said as he perched on the porch railing. "How's your head feel today?"

"Marvelous. Thanks for your prayers. I'm sure that had a lot to do with my healing."

With a pen, Ryan drew a hand on the cast. He put a ring on the fourth finger. "That's for intercessory prayer. I learned all about that last week."

"And you learned a lot about responsibility too. You've worked hard since I got banged up, and now it's time for you to have some fun. Pete's going to take you

101

camping and fishing."

"Are we staying overnight?"

"You got it. Hand me my crutches, please." Grady lifted his cast off the pillows. "We haven't much time to pack your gear."

At four o'clock in the afternoon, Pete and Ryan set out for the high country. After an hour's ride, they came to a small lake.

Pete called over his shoulder, "This is my favorite fishing spot. We'll camp here."

They took the packs and saddles off the horses. Then they gathered wood for a fire.

Pete unpacked his fishing gear. "Let's catch our dinner. Have you been practicing like I showed you?"

"Sure have." Ryan tied a fly on his line.

"That's a good knot," Pete said. With smooth action, he cast a tight loop behind him, then laid the fishing line out on the lake. After a few minutes he reeled in a trout.

"Wow! You're good," Ryan exclaimed.

"Well, I've been fishing as long as I've been walking. I should have these trout figured out by now."

Pete watched Ryan's casting. "Relax, let the rod do the work," he advised.

To Ryan's delight, he finally landed his first rainbow trout. When they'd caught two apiece, they gutted them and then washed them in the lake.

"I'll build the fire," said Pete. "You put some butter, salt, and pepper inside the fish and roll them in foil."

After dinner, Pete played some Western songs on his harmonica. Ryan hummed along, singing the parts he knew.

"Tell me about the first rodeo you were in, Pete," Ryan said.

"Well now, that goes back a few years. My dad owned the ranch right next to Hidden Haven, which, of course, belonged to your grandfather. My best friends were Grady and your dad. We loved horses, practically lived on them. Winter or summer. Didn't make any difference to us. People called us the Western Musketeers."

Pete broke a branch over his knee and threw the pieces into the fire.

"As kids, we entered every horse show that came to town. When we got to be teenagers, we rode in our first rodeo."

"When did you start winning?" Ryan asked.

"I didn't win anything that first year or the second. Actually, your dad collected more ribbons and trophies and cash than either Grady or I did."

"My dad? My dad was a rodeo winner?"

"More than once." Pete poked the fire with a long stick. "You must have known that."

"No, I didn't. Dad only told stories about you and Uncle Grady."

"I think it's time for you to hear his story. When your dad was twenty-one years old, he was thrown from a bucking bronco, just like Grady was last week. Only he wasn't so lucky. He hurt his back, really bad! The doctors said he'd never walk again."

Ryan fixed his eyes on Pete.

"But your dad was as tough as any cowboy I've ever known. He was determined to walk. And he did. But he's never been the same."

"I didn't know." Ryan stared into the fire. "Dad never told me anything about it."

"He gave up ranching and riding. He had no choice. Even today, when he stands or walks, he's in constant pain."

Ryan picked up a skinny branch. He broke it into lots of tiny pieces, slowly tossing them one by one into the fire.

"That's why my dad's got an office job. That's why he doesn't play softball with me, or take me horseback riding, or go fishing."

Ryan sat on a log and let the tears roll freely down his face.

"I'm going to check on the horses," said Pete, disappearing into the darkness.

When he came back, Ryan was poking the fire.

"What can I do to help my dad?"

"If I were you, I'd tell your dad that you know all about it, that you understand, that he doesn't have to act brave anymore." Pete paused. "And you can pray for your dad."

Ryan peeled the bark off a small branch. "I guess I've been pretty selfish. I always asked God for things I wanted."

"Lots of folks make that mistake, praying for things instead of people."

"Last week I learned a lot about interceding. I was a go-between for Uncle Grady, and I believe it worked. Maybe it'll work for my dad, too."

"I think it will," Pete said quietly.

"Uncle Grady told me God hears our prayers no matter where we are. Do you think I can pray here by the campfire?"

"Sure can," said Pete. "And there's no rule that says you always have to kneel or close your eyes when you pray."

Ryan stared into the dying fire. "Dear God," he began. "I'm glad You're always listening. I'm really glad that I can talk to You any place, any time. Thanks for this camping trip and for Pete. Thank You for letting me find this out about my dad. Forgive me for being selfish. I haven't thought much about other people's problems. Please help my dad right now. Take away some of his pain and make him happy again. Amen."

With a shovel of dirt, Pete smothered the burning coals. The two campers unrolled their sleeping bags and crawled inside. Sleep came quickly to Ryan as he gazed at the stars above him and breathed in the cold mountain air.

TO THINK ABOUT

I urge, then, first of all, that requests, prayers, intercession and thanksgiving be made for everyone— for kings and all those in authority, that we may live peaceful and quiet lives in all godliness and holiness. This is good, and pleases God our Savior. (1 Timothy 2:1-3)

TO TALK ABOUT

1. According to Paul's letter to Timothy, who are we to pray for?
2. How does God feel when you become a go-between for leaders?
3. a. Why hadn't Ryan prayed for other people before?
   b. What did Ryan discover about the way he used to pray?

TO DO

1. Make a list of some people "in authority" that you can pray for in your home, school, church, town, country.
2. Using your list, make several Asking for Others Cards. Don't forget your own family. Here are some ideas:

ASKING FOR OTHERS

Please encourage Pastor Ferguson each day. Make him wise and strong. Make him loving and kind so he can help others.

ASKING FOR OTHERS

Lord, my teacher, Mrs. Graham, has a hard job trying to teach us kids everyday. Give her patience and wisdom. Fill her heart with Your love so she can love us.

ASKING FOR SELF

Chapter 15

GREEN EYES IN THE BARN

"Your cast and crutches are getting muddy," Ryan told his uncle. "You'd better go back to the porch. I can feed these heifers alone."

"That rain last night turned this feeding pen into a mud hole." Uncle Grady looked down at his crutches. "Oh, my! Marta will think I'm more bother than I'm worth. You're right. It's back to the recliner for me."

With Uncle Grady on crutches, Ryan's responsibilities had increased. The job he liked best was feeding the white-faced yearling heifers his uncle was fattening for market.

At first Ryan was going to name the heifers, but then he changed his mind. After all, they weren't pets, and he didn't want to get attached to them. Raising calves and selling them for beef was the way Uncle

Grady and Aunt Marta earned a living.

Ryan found a shovel hanging on the barn wall. Unlatching the door to the grain room, he went in and filled two buckets with corn. He carried them out to the pen behind the barn.

Standing on the lowest fence rail, Ryan leaned over the top of the fence and filled the two wooden feed troughs with corn.

Two more trips and that job will be done, thought Ryan.

While walking through the barn, he got an eerie feeling that someone was watching him. After tossing the buckets into the grain room, he picked up the shovel and looked all around.

"Who's here?" he called.

He didn't see anyone. But he heard something.

"S-s-s sp-t! S-s-s sp-t!"

He looked up. From the haymow two green eyes ringed with fire stared at him.

A stray cat, Ryan thought, tossing a stick at it.

It moved out from behind the bales of hay, and Ryan got a better view. *That's no ordinary cat,* Ryan thought. *It's much too big.*

The cat hunched its back. Its roughed-up fur was covered with blotches. Its big ears had long tufts of hair sticking out on the pointed ends.

And its tail? Ryan squinted his eyes. It looked like someone had chopped it off.

112

The cat crept along the edge of the haymow, coming closer and closer. When it was right by Ryan, the cat stood still and crouched, ready to spring. It showed its long canine teeth and made that spitting sound again.

Ryan tightened his grip on the handle of the shovel until his knuckles turned white. He could feel the sweat dripping down his forehead. He tried to move, but his feet were glued to the floor.

"Please, God," he whispered, squeezing his eyes shut. "Please help me."

When he opened his eyes, he saw the short tail disappear behind the hay.

Unwrapping his clenched fingers from the handle, Ryan carefully laid the shovel down. Slowly and quietly, he backed out the barn door.

Turning quickly, he made a beeline for the house, not once looking back for fear he might see that long-legged, green-eyed cat gaining on him.

Ryan stumbled up the porch steps, gasping for breath.

"What's wrong?" asked Uncle Grady. "You ran like a grizzly bear was chasing you."

"It's in the barn! I saw it in the barn."

"A grizzly bear?" Uncle Grady teased.

After Ryan described the strange-looking cat, Grady said, "That's a bobcat. They can be fierce little animals."

"Do they attack people?" Ryan asked.

"Only if they feel cornered."

Pete drove up in the pickup and hollered, "I'm going to the west pasture to drop some salt blocks. Anyone want to come along?"

Uncle Grady grabbed his crutches. "We've got another job to do first. Ryan saw a bobcat in the barn. We don't want it stealing our chickens."

Ryan felt safe, walking between Pete with a shotgun and Uncle Grady with crutches.

Pete climbed up the ladder into the haymow. He

searched among the bales while Uncle Grady poked around on the ground floor. Ryan watched from the barn door.

"He's gone," said Pete, coming down the ladder. "He probably just came in to get out of the rainstorm last night."

"I doubt that he'll be back." With a crutch, Uncle Grady poked at the shovel lying on the floor. "What's this doing in the middle of the barn? Someone could trip over it."

Picking up the shovel, Ryan asked, "Want to help me finish my job, Pete? Then I'll help you with those salt blocks."

"It's a deal," said Pete.

TO THINK ABOUT

How gracious he will be when you cry for help! As soon as he hears, he will answer you.

(Isaiah 30:19)

TO TALK ABOUT

1. According to Isaiah 30:19, how soon will God answer our cry for help?
2. Do you think God heard Ryan's cry for help? Why or why not?
3. a. Talk about a time you prayed to God because you were scared or in danger.
   b. What happened when you prayed?

TO DO

1. Check the list of people you made in your last session and make more Asking for Others Cards.
2. Have you put a symbol on each card and colored the border?

Chapter 16

SHORT PRAYERS COUNT TOO

Ryan and Uncle Grady were gazing at the stars when Aunt Marta joined them on the back porch. Sitting on the swing, she said, "I hear you had quite an adventure today."

Perched on the porch railing, Ryan told her about the piercing green eyes, the tufts of hair on the bobcat's ears, and his own fear.

"How wonderful!" Aunt Marta exclaimed. "God answered your prayer."

"Prayer? What prayer?" Ryan asked.

"When you whispered, 'God, please help me.'"

"That counts as a prayer?" Ryan was surprised. "I was too scared to think. The words just came out."

"I've prayed like that," Aunt Marta admitted. "I call that a quickie prayer."

Ryan frowned. "But I thought I had to say all the parts you've been teaching me."

"Short prayers count too," Uncle Grady added. He was carefully carving a crude-looking cowboy out of wood. "Even great men of the Bible have prayed like you did."

"Really? Who?"

"Nehemiah, for one."

"Who's he?"

"An important man in Jewish history," Uncle Grady said. "In fact, there's an entire book of the Bible about him."

Aunt Marta went into the house.

Uncle Grady continued, "Nehemiah was an officer, serving in the palace of the King of Persia. One day Nehemiah heard that his people back in Jerusalem were in trouble."

"What kind of trouble?"

Uncle Grady brushed the wood chips off his jeans. "In those days cities had big walls around them to keep the enemies out. But the walls of Jerusalem had been broken down and the gates burned. Nehemiah wanted to go and help, but he was afraid to ask the king for permission. So he fasted and prayed for several days."

"Stop!" Ryan held up his hand like a policeman directing traffic. "You call that a quickie prayer?"

"Be patient. I'm getting to that."

118

Aunt Marta returned with her Bible. And Uncle Grady continued his story. "One day the king asked Nehemiah, 'Why do you look so sad?' Nehemiah answered, 'Because the city where my ancestors are buried is in ruins, and the gates have been burned.'"

Aunt Marta handed her open Bible to Ryan. "You can find out what Nehemiah did next, in chapter 2, verses 4 and 5."

Ryan read aloud: "The king said to me, 'What is it you want?' Then I prayed to the God of heaven, and I answered the king . . ."

119

"Stop!" Uncle Grady grinned and held out his hand. "Do you think Nehemiah had time for all five parts of prayer before he answered the king?"

"I doubt it," said Ryan, sitting down on the swing beside his aunt. "I bet he said, 'Help me, God.'"

"And God did. The king sent Nehemiah to Jerusalem to organize the people and rebuild the walls. Things were going just fine. But the enemy tried to scare the people so they wouldn't finish the job."

"What happened?"

Aunt Marta read verse 9 of chapter 6. "But I prayed, 'Now strengthen my hands.'"

Ryan grinned. "That's another quickie like mine. I like this guy, Nehemiah."

Closing her Bible, Aunt Marta went inside.

Uncle Grady folded in the blade of his pocket knife and slid it into his pocket. "I think there's a secret to getting short prayers answered."

Ryan raised his eyebrows. "A secret?"

"Nehemiah obeyed God. He praised God a lot and talked to him often. God heard and answered his long prayers. And his short ones, too."

"Cold drinks are ready," called Aunt Marta from inside the house.

Inside, Ryan sat down with Uncle Grady at the round oak table. "I'm sure glad to learn God hears quickie prayers for help."

"And you've learned one more thing." Marta carried the tray of drinks to the table. "You've learned the fifth and last ingredient of prayer."

Ryan sipped the cold punch. "I have?"

"The tiny finger on the praying hands reminds us to ask for help for ourselves."

"It's taken all summer to get to the only kind of prayer I ever prayed," Ryan said. "Except, I'm learning that asking for self means much more than asking for things I want—like a bicycle."

Ryan hugged his aunt. "Thanks for this fruit punch—and for teaching me how to talk to God."

TO THINK ABOUT

"Call upon me in the day of trouble;
I will deliver you, and you will honor me."

(Psalm 50:15)

TO TALK ABOUT

1. According to Psalm 50:15, what should we do when we are in trouble?
2. a. When God helps us, what should we do?
   b. Can you think of ways to honor Him?
3. What did Uncle Grady say was the secret to getting quickie prayers answered?
4. What is the fifth ingredient of prayer?
5. Nehemiah often asked God to help him with his problems. What other Bible characters asked God for help?

121

TO DO

1. Make some Asking for Self Cards. Ask God to help you with your problems. Here are some ideas:
   - Getting along with someone
   - School lessons
   - Chores around the house
2. Here is a sample card:

ASKING FOR MYSELF
God, I have a problem getting
along with _____. Please
help me be kind even when I
don't feel like it. And help
me to be careful what I say.

Chapter 17

A CHALLENGE AT THE COUNTY FAIR

The August sun was peeking over the eastern ridge as the Bennett's pickup pulled into the Archuleta County fair grounds. Kevin and Ryan were riding in the bed of the truck, along with a pig and a steer.

"Why did we come so early?" Ryan yawned.

"The hog show begins at eight o'clock," said Kevin. "My sis has to get Porky ready for judging."

"Get a pig ready? What's that mean?" asked Ryan as the pickup stopped in front of the livestock barn.

"You'll see. Porky will be beautiful when Kristin gets done with him."

Kristin climbed out of the cab and let down the tailgate. "Will you guys help me get Porky into the grooming barn? I've only got an hour and a half before the judging begins."

"Sure," said Kevin. "The steer show isn't until ten o'clock."

Thirty minutes later, Ryan watched Kristin in her black rubber boots hosing down Porky. Water and soap suds ran down the drain in the cement floor. When Kristin finished, Porky's coarse gray hair lay smooth and dry. His pink ears shone. His hoofs were spotless.

"I've never seen such a clean pig before," Ryan said, laughing. "What's next?"

"I'll put Porky in his stall, change my clothes, and comb this mop of mine." Kristin pushed her long brown hair away from her face. "Then I'll wait for my turn to show him off to the judges."

"He's a good-looking pig." Ryan leaned over the rail and gave Porky a pat. "Yuk! He feels like my mom's scrub brush."

Ryan jumped off the rail. "I'm going to find Kevin."

Wandering through the rabbit shed, Ryan saw boys and girls and rabbits everywhere.

"Hey, Ryan!" It was Holly, one of the kids from Sunday school, struggling with four rabbits.

"Here, hold one for me." She shoved her floppy-eared doe into Ryan's arms.

"What long, soft fur." It reminded Ryan of the white fluffy stuff on dandelions going to seed.

"She just had a bath this morning." Holly put water and pellets into the cages.

Walking through the poultry shed was a noisy experience. Every chicken was cackling or flapping its wings. Ryan couldn't wait to get out of there.

In the big barn, Ryan stopped to look at sheep and goats, cows and horses. He found Kevin sitting on the rail in front of his own steer.

"Where've you been?" asked Kevin. "We've gotta get over to the hog judging, pronto."

The boys watched the judge award Kristin a blue ribbon, as well as the Best of Breed ribbon. Back at the stall, Kristin proudly hung up the ribbons. Porky lay down. He seemed to be glad the fuss was over.

Later, Kevin's steer took a white ribbon for third place.

The boys met Kristin for lunch under the red and white striped tent. One large Pepsi and two hot dogs smothered in mustard and heaped with pickle relish satisfied Ryan's thirst and his growling stomach.

"What's next?" he asked.

"How about some carnival rides?" suggested Kristin.

"Great idea." Sweat was running down Ryan's neck. "Is it always this hot at county fairs?"

"Yup, but I know how to cool you off." Kevin chuckled as he dumped his cup of ice down Ryan's shirt.

The twins snickered while Ryan sucked in his breath and danced a jig. He jerked his shirt away from his back and let the ice fall out.

"Do we have to pay to see this clown perform?" The sneering voice belonged to Danny Hathaway. He grabbed a chair, turned it around, and sat down backwards.

Kristin's smile turned into a frown. "I'll meet you guys at the ferris wheel." She threw her napkin and cup into the trash can and left.

"Want to join us?" Kevin asked politely.

"Suppose so." Danny shrugged and wrinkled his nose. "Nothing else to do in this boring place."

The three boys joined the pushing, pressing crowd of people in the midway. In front of the Ferris wheel, Ryan spied a wallet in their path.

"Look what I found," he said, picking it up.

It was crammed with credit cards and lots of money.

"Finders keepers!" said Danny. "Let's count it."

Behind a horse trailer they sat down and counted the bills. Four ones, two tens, and five twenties.

"That's over a hundred dollars!" Ryan gasped.

"Keep the money," said Danny, "and toss the wallet under this trailer."

"But—but, it isn't mine," stuttered Ryan.

"It is now. You found it." Danny leaned against Ryan and whispered into his ear. "Think what you could do with all that money."

"I've got an idea." Kevin glanced to see if anyone

was coming. "Keep the money and turn in the wallet. After all, the person needs his credit cards and driver's license."

"That's true," said Ryan. "He'd be glad to get those back. Someone else might not return anything. I deserve a reward for doing that."

"Hurry up," Danny ordered, poking Ryan in the side. "Take the money out before someone sees us."

"Hi, guys! What're you doing back here?" Kristin asked, seeming to appear out of nowhere.

Ryan shoved the wallet into his pocket.

Kevin jumped up. "Just—waiting for you. Let's ride the spinning tubs."

While the spinning tubs went round and round, Ryan's mind was on the money in the wallet. He could buy that bike he'd been praying for. In fact, maybe God let him find the wallet on purpose.

After the spinning tubs, they rode the flying airplanes. Ryan kept thinking about the money. Right when he thought he had it all figured out, a voice whispered inside his head: *That's called stealing.*

Ryan's insides were turned upside down, but not from the airplane ride.

During the horse pulling contest, Danny kept poking him, urging him to "Do it now, man!"

The quiet voice said, *Don't listen to him.*

While people were cheering and stomping their feet, Ryan prayed silently, "Dear God, please make me strong, so I can do the right thing."

About four o'clock, Ryan let out a sigh of relief. "Take me to the lost-and-found tent," he whispered in Kevin's ear. "I'm turning in the wallet with everything in it."

Kevin smiled. "I thought you would."

"You're stupid," Danny snarled.

"I sure was tempted," Ryan admitted to Kevin, as they left the grandstand. "But I know this is the right thing to do. And I feel good about it."

TO THINK ABOUT

For God is at work within you, helping you want to obey him, and then helping you do what he wants. (Philippians 2:13, TLB)

TO TALK ABOUT

1. a. Have any of your friends tried to influence you to do something you know is wrong? What was it?
   b. What happened?
2. Do you think Ryan is getting stronger in his character? Why or why not?
3. If you memorize the promise in Philippians 2:13, how will that make you a stronger Christian?

TO DO

1. Make Asking for Self Cards to help you become a better person. Choose some Scripture references

below to read aloud and talk about. Then write
your own Asking for Self Cards.
- Psalm 86:11
- Psalm 139:23
- Proverbs 3:5-6
- Matthew 7:12
- Matthew 22:37-39
- Ephesians 4:25,29,32
- Ephesians 6:1

2. On his Asking for Self Cards, Ryan drew a green
pine tree to remind him that praying these verses
will help him grow stronger in character. Color the
borders and draw a symbol on your cards.

PUTTING IT ALL
TOGETHER

Chapter 18

CRUTCHES AREN'T FOREVER

"My back is breaking!" Ryan groaned.

Slowly he straightened up, stretched, and wiped his sweaty forehead with the back of his hand.

Across the bean patch, he could see Aunt Marta bent over a row of beans. *I shouldn't complain,* he thought. *She's been picking in the hot sun all morning.*

With his foot he shoved the yellow plastic tub ahead of him. Bending over, he held the bushy plant to one side and pulled off the long green beans hanging from the stems.

Soon he heard his aunt call, "Let's quit. We've picked enough to keep me busy all afternoon."

Ryan carried the bushel basket of beans to the kitchen. Then the two sat down at the table to enjoy

133

tall glasses of iced tea.

"When will Pete and Uncle Grady get back from town?" Ryan asked, as he built a five-story ham-and-cheese sandwich.

"The doctor has to take an X-ray of Grady's foot to see if it's healing properly. Pete has several errands to run. They won't be home till dinner."

When Ryan took a bite of his sandwich, a tomato slice scooted out. He shoved it back. "Maybe I can help you with the beans."

"I won't refuse an offer like that," Aunt Marta said, turning on the television. "Let's watch the baseball game while we work."

"You like baseball?"

"Love it! I was in a women's softball league for years, when I was younger. I played shortstop."

The Cubs were playing, Ryan's favorite team. And they were leading the Cardinals 3 to 2.

After washing the beans, Ryan snapped off the ends. He quickly discovered that he could watch the game and break beans without even looking at them.

After the Cubs won 5 to 4, Ryan turned off the TV.

"I'm done snapping beans," he said, surprised that the afternoon had gone so quickly. "What's next?"

"You've done enough." Aunt Marta said as she dumped another batch of beans into the boiling water. "Thanks for your help."

Ryan carried the yellow tub of beans to the sink. "I've been meaning to ask you a question about the prayer cards. Now that I've made cards for all five parts, what do I do with them?"

"If you'll get your cards, I'll show you while I bag these beans for the freezer."

Ryan returned with his box of prayer cards. He put them in five stacks according to their colored borders.

"Take one card from each stack," suggested Marta, "and arrange them in the order of the fingers on the praying hands."

Ryan laid five cards in a row: Praising, Thanking, Confessing, Asking for Others, and Asking for Self.

"Remember, we said attitude was important," Aunt Marta said. "So be quiet for a moment, and think about God. Then read your cards."

Ryan read the five cards aloud. "I feel funny reading a prayer."

"That's normal at first." Aunt Marta was sealing a plastic bag full of green beans. "Why don't you choose five new ones and try again? When you finish, close your prayer by saying, 'I ask this in the name of Jesus.'"

Ryan read the second set silently. "That was easier. I like the way they fit together. How long will I have to read from these cards?"

"I'll let you answer that. How long will Uncle Grady

walk with his crutches?"

Ryan thought for a moment. He broke into a grin and said, "Until he can get along without them, I guess."

Collecting his cards, Ryan put them back into the box.

Pete opened the screen door and called out, "We're home."

In walked Grady, carrying his crutches. "I have to keep the cast on for two more weeks, but I don't need my crutches any longer." He handed them to Ryan.

Ryan put a crutch under each arm. Winking at his aunt, he said, "I'm sure glad to know that crutches aren't forever."

TO THINK ABOUT

Very early in the morning, while it was still dark, Jesus got up, left the house and went off to a solitary place, where he prayed. (Mark 1:35)

TO TALK ABOUT:

1. a. Sometimes people say, "I'm too busy to pray." What was Jesus busy doing?
   b. When did He find time to pray?
   c. Where did He pray?
2. a. Which of the five ingredients do you think Jesus included in His prayers?
   b. What do you think He said to God?

3. What did Marta suggest Ryan do before he prays?
4. How are the prayer cards like crutches?

TO DO

1. Practice using your prayer cards.
   a. Stack them according to the colored borders.
   b. Select one from each stack.
   c. Place them in the proper order. Remember your five fingers: Praising, Thanking, Confessing, Asking for Others, Asking for Self.
   d. Each person can read his or her set of cards.
2. You can use the cards for a family prayer too. Assign one (or two) of the five ingredients to each family member. Each person reads his or her card in turn. Close by saying, "We ask this in Jesus' name. Amen."

Chapter 19

THE PERFECT EXAMPLE

Ryan curried and brushed Rustler longer than usual. "That's the last grooming you'll get from me this summer," he said, slapping Rustler on the rump. "Go on now. Join the other horses in the pasture."

He put the saddle in the tack room. He'd miss this old barn with its special smells—the leather, the horses and hay, the pine shavings, and even the manure.

In the corral Uncle Grady was repairing the gate.

"Tomorrow I go back to the city," Ryan said sadly.

"You've been a big help this summer," said Uncle Grady. "I don't think I could have gotten along without you. In fact, you've become quite a responsible young man."

Ryan climbed up on the fence. "It feels good to be

responsible. And I've grown in another way too. Thanks for teaching me about prayer."

"Learning to talk to God is important if you want Him to be your helper and friend."

"I still have one question I'd like to ask before I go," Ryan said.

Uncle Grady laid down his tools. "My foot needs a rest. Let's sit under the old cottonwood down by the creek."

Under the tree Ryan said, "I've been using my prayer cards every morning. And it's been working fine. But . . ." He picked up a stone and tossed it into the creek. "Do I have to say all five parts every time I pray?"

Awkwardly, Uncle Grady sat down on the ground. "Not always. Sometimes you feel like praising and thanking God. Sometimes you want to pray for people. Even when you use all five ingredients, they might be in a different order. Aunt Marta taught you a prayer pattern. But you can adjust it to suit each situation."

"That's good," Ryan said. He took off his cowboy hat. Sprawling on the ground, he put his hands under his head.

"Let me tell you about the perfect example," Uncle Grady said as he leaned back against the tree. His hat slid down, resting on his nose. "I'm sure you've heard it before. It's the Lord's Prayer."

"*Our Father which art in heaven,*" Ryan began.

"Begin reverently," Uncle Grady said. "God is our Father. We should come to Him as obedient and loving children."

"*Hallowed be thy name*," Ryan continued. "I say that, but I don't know what it means."

"God is holy. We worship and honor Him. And we want men everywhere to treat God's holy name with deep respect. Next?" prompted Grady.

"*Thy kingdom come. Thy will be done in earth, as it is in heaven*," Ryan said.

"That's praising. We're saying, 'God, You are the King and Ruler over everything. We want everyone on earth to obey You, just as the beings in Heaven do.'"

"*Give us this day our daily bread*." Ryan sat up. "That part's easy. We're asking God to give us the food we need."

"Right," said Uncle Grady. "What does the next line mean: *And forgive us our debts, as we forgive our debtors?*"

"That's confessing." Ryan grabbed a low branch and pulled himself up into the tree. "I understand this part. *Debts* are sins. It's when I disobey God, like when I lied to you. *Debtors* are people who have done something bad to me, like Danny when he tried to make me steal that money."

"God wants us to confess our sins and ask Him to forgive us," Uncle Grady said. "He also wants us to forgive people who hurt us."

Ryan continued: "*And lead us not into temptation, but deliver us from evil.*"

"When you pray this line, you're asking God to keep you out of trouble, to make you strong in character so you won't sin."

"That's happened to me," Ryan said, remembering the wallet at the county fair.

"Jesus closed His prayer by praising God again," said Uncle Grady.

"*For thine is the kingdom, and the power, and the glory, for ever,*" Ryan quoted. He dropped out of the tree, and jumped over Grady's cast.

Grady flinched and his hat fell off. "You've got more energy than a scared jackrabbit. Did you hear anything I said?"

"Sure did," Ryan said with a smile. "Test me."

Uncle Grady stuck his hat over his cast as if to protect his foot. "Which of the five ingredients are in the Lord's Prayer?"

"Let's see." Ryan frowned and his brown freckles wrinkled. "Confessing and asking were in the middle."

"What about the opening and closing?"

"It starts with praising, and it ends with praising."

"Right! Praising is important," Uncle Grady said. "Don't ever leave that ingredient out of your prayer."

The clanging cowbell sounded faraway.

"I won't hear that sound in the city," Ryan said, as he reached out and pulled his uncle up.

"How about coming back next summer? We could even work out an allowance for your ranching chores."

"Really?" Picking up his borrowed hat, Ryan affectionately stroked the brim before he put it on. "You mean I'd be considered a cowhand?"

"I've got a lot of time and training invested in you. I don't want to lose that."

Slowly and smoothly Uncle Grady winked his left eye, without scrunching his nose, or wrinkling his cheek, or wiggling his moustache.

"You finally got it!" Ryan cheered and did a little victory dance.

Uncle Grady put a hand on Ryan's shoulder, and the two cowboys walked up the hill to dinner.

TO THINK ABOUT
And lead us not into temptation, but deliver us from evil. (Matthew 6:13, KJV)

TO TALK ABOUT
1. Put the verse above in your own words. What do we mean by the word *temptation*?
2. Proverbs 1:10 says: "My son, if sinners entice you, do not give in to them." Was there a time you were tempted to do something wrong, but you said "No!" Share it with your family. Sharing makes you stronger and helps family members understand each other better.

143

TO DO

1. Make one more Asking for Self Card by rewriting the verse above (Matthew 6:13) from the Lord's Prayer.
2. Here's an extra project.

   Read Nehemiah's prayer in Nehemiah 1:5-10. Nehemiah used three of the ingredients of prayer: praising (two times), confessing, asking for self (two times). Find them.

Chapter 20

GOODBYE, SUMMER

"This airport is friendly, not scary like O'Hare International in Chicago," said Ryan. His blue backpack was strapped over his shoulder.

"Yup. Small and friendly." Pete walked beside him carrying two large bags. "You can't get lost here, but you can't fly far, either. You'll have to transfer to another airline in Denver."

At the ticket window, Ryan checked his baggage through to Chicago. Then he asked for a seat by the window.

I hate goodbyes, Ryan thought.

Pete grabbed Ryan's hand and shook it vigorously. "Here's something to read on the plane." It was an illustrated book on fly fishing.

"I guess we had the same idea," said Uncle Grady,

145

giving Ryan a hearty hug and a *Western Horseman* magazine.

"Not me," said Aunt Marta. "Here's a box of my favorite pecan fudge." She gave him a kiss and her customary pat on the cheek.

Ryan didn't mind. She was a very special person.

"Flight 102 to Denver is now boarding." Ryan heard the announcement over the airport sound system.

"Hey! Ryan! Wait a minute." Kevin and Kristin Bennett raced across the terminal. They were dressed alike in yellow Western shirts. They did that only for special occasions.

"We want to say goodbye, too," said Kevin. "It's been great having you here all summer. I hope you can come back next year."

"Me, too," said Ryan.

Kristin tucked a small envelope into Ryan's shirt pocket. "You can open it on the plane."

"Thanks, everyone, for everything," Ryan said. He walked through the revolving door and out to the plane. As he climbed the stairs, he turned and waved goodbye.

Settled in his seat, he tasted the fudge. No wonder Aunt Marta called it her favorite.

When Ryan opened Kristin's envelope, he found a photo of her and Porky with his two blue ribbons. She was wearing a pink shirt. Her brown hair hung in soft waves around her face. On the back, she had written, "With special memories of good times together. Your summer friend, Kristin."

He smiled as he remembered Kristin scrubbing the pig, catching trout, riding bareback. *What a girl! And she's pretty, too*, he thought, putting the photo in his wallet.

He looked out the window. As far as he could see, jagged mountains filled the blue sky. Above the peaks drifted puffy white clouds.

Ryan put his head back on the tall seat and closed his eyes.

"Dear God," he prayed silently. "What a beautiful world You have made.

"Thanks for letting me spend the summer in Colorado. And thanks for my aunt and uncle who taught me how to talk to You. I feel like we're getting to be friends, Lord.

"I'm really sorry that my prayers were so selfish before. From now on, I'm going to change that.

"Please make Uncle Grady's leg and foot strong again. And be with Aunt Marta when she's teaching kids each Sunday.

"Now I'm going home. Teach me how to show Dad I understand, and that I really love and care about him.

"And one more thing, Lord. School's about to start. Please make me strong so I can do what's right, even when I'm with kids who want to do wrong.

"I ask all this in Jesus' name. Amen."

Ryan reached for another piece of fudge. *No doubt about it. This has been my best summer ever!*

TO THINK ABOUT

Don't be weary in prayer; keep at it; watch for God's answers and remember to be thankful when they come. (Colossians 4:2, TLB)

TO TALK ABOUT:

1. a. Identify the parts of Ryan's prayer.
   b. Did he include all five ingredients?
2. What new friends did Ryan make this summer?
3. The verse above reminds us to thank God when He answers prayer. What prayers has God answered for you?

   Sharing with others will make your faith stronger. God likes to hear it, too. When you tell others what God has done for you, that's a form of praise.

TO DO

Spend some time now praying together as a family. See what comes out in simply talking to God, as Ryan did, without prayer cards.